The Laziest

THE BROWN BEAR

THE ORANGUTAN

THE GRASS SNAKE

THE ALPINE MARMOT

THE THREE-TOED SLOTH

THE COW

THE HIPPOPOTAMUS

THE CAT

THE GARDEN DORMOUSE

THE LESSER HORSESHOE BAT

THE EDIBLE SNAIL

THE FLAMINGO

RANDOM HOUSE · NEW YORK

The Brown BEAR

Address: North America, Europe, and Asia

Size: From 7 to 10 feet long

Weight: From 300 to over 1,000 pounds

Favorite food: Grubs, blueberries, and honey

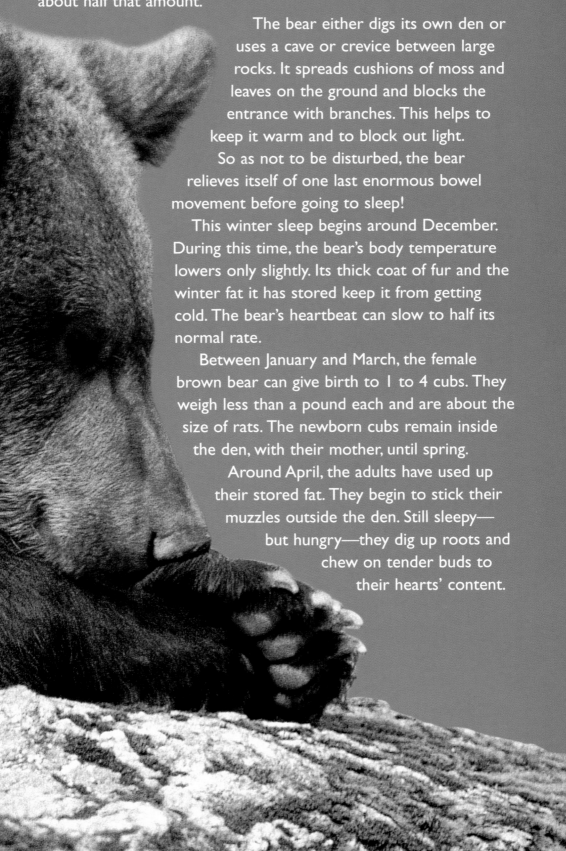

During its 5-month-long winter nap, this giant of the mountains loses over 100 pounds. . . .

In the fall, the brown bear fattens up to prepare for its winter sleep. Every night, it can eat up to 40 pounds of moisture-rich plants, tubers, and berries. Sometimes it dines on carrion or fishes for trout or salmon from a river. After gorging like this, the male brown bear can weigh almost 1,000 pounds. The female can weigh about half that amount.

The bear either digs its own den or uses a cave or crevice between large rocks. It spreads cushions of moss and leaves on the ground and blocks the entrance with branches. This helps to keep it warm and to block out light.

So as not to be disturbed, the bear relieves itself of one last enormous bowel movement before going to sleep!

This winter sleep begins around December. During this time, the bear's body temperature lowers only slightly. Its thick coat of fur and the winter fat it has stored keep it from getting cold. The bear's heartbeat can slow to half its normal rate.

Between January and March, the female brown bear can give birth to 1 to 4 cubs. They weigh less than a pound each and are about the size of rats. The newborn cubs remain inside the den, with their mother, until spring.

Around April, the adults have used up their stored fat. They begin to stick their muzzles outside the den. Still sleepy— but hungry—they dig up roots and chew on tender buds to their hearts' content.

The Orangutan

For this lazybones, a good night's sleep requires . . . a good mattress! The orangutan makes itself a new bed every day.

Asia

Address: The islands of Sumatra and Borneo in Southeast Asia

Size: Male: About 5 feet long
Female: About 4 feet long

Weight: Male: About 175–200 pounds
Female: About 90 pounds

Favorite food: Fruit

But making a proper bed takes time! That's why the orangutan makes its bed every day before sunset. Some 50 to 65 feet above the ground in the treetops, the male orangutan searches for a good location by swinging on the branches. He must find a spot strong enough to hold his 200-pound body for 14 hours!

After finding a suitable branch, the orangutan takes great care to make a comfortable bed. He uses his long arms (which reach down to his ankles) to grab at leafy vines hanging in the trees. The orangutan then piles them into a soft mattress on his branch.

The female orangutan makes a comfy bed off by herself and sleeps with her baby. There's no need for a cradle, however! The baby sleeps clutching its mother's fur.

(The baby is doted on and will be breast-fed until it is 3½ years old. The mother orangutan will also feed her baby solid food that she has chewed into a mash.)

In the morning—refreshed from a good night's sleep—the orangutans then groom one another for hours.

The Grass Snake

Address: Europe, North Africa, and western Asia

Size: 2 to 5 feet long

Favorite food: Small fish, toads, and salamanders

In early April, this lazy reptile awakens from a sleep that's lasted over 150 days!

Still sluggish with cold, the grass snake uncoils its three-and-a-half-foot-long body. It spends hours basking in the sun, increasing its body temperature to that of a warm-blooded animal.

Then . . . it's time to freshen up! As the grass snake grows, it sheds its skin 5 to 7 times a year. A new skin grows underneath the old one. When the time is right, all the snake has to do is move slowly forward and it slithers out of the old skin!

Harmless to humans, grass snakes are preyed upon by hawks and other raptors. But when danger threatens, this snake doesn't panic—it plays dead! Remaining completely motionless with its tongue hanging out, the grass snake secretes a foul-smelling liquid. This technique keeps predators away, without the snake's having to move a muscle!

From late fall until spring, the grass snake's priority is to keep warm. Snakes do not like cold weather. For warmth, the grass snakes gather together in a tree trunk or under a rock. They coil themselves around each other like a mound of spaghetti and sleep this way until the following spring.

The Alpine Marmot

For 5 to 6 months, this rodent sleeps soundly (waking only every three weeks to use the bathroom)!

In the mountains in Europe at an altitude of 8,000 feet, winter comes early. By mid-October, outside temperatures drop below 54°F. In their burrows, alpine marmots prepare a thick bed of straw. They plug up the entrance with a big clump of grass, earth, and stone.

France

Massif Central mountains

The Alps

The Pyrénées

Address: The Alps, the Pyrénées, and the Massif Central mountains in France

Size: From 17 to 23 inches long, plus a 6-to-8-inch-long tail

Weight: From 6 to 17 pounds

Favorite food: Clover, wild-carrot flowers, and blueberries

Rolled into a ball, the marmots save energy by—guess what?—sleeping! The members of an entire marmot family (which may include up to 15 animals) huddle close together with their noses between their hind legs. During hibernation, their body temperature can drop from 98.6°F to 39°F. If it drops below 39°F, the marmots wake up and wiggle their feet. This causes their temperature to rise, and they quickly fall back asleep.

Marmots live on stored body fat throughout their hibernation. When spring comes, they eat like pigs for about 6 months— doubling their weight to ready themselves for another hibernation!

The Three-Toed Sloth

The least stressed-out of all mammals sleeps for 10 out of 24 hours! Even when it's awake, it looks as if it's moving in slow motion. . . .

During its sleep, the sloth always maintains the same position. With its head upside down, it hangs from branches by its 3 long, clawed toes. When it is not sleeping, this vegetarian eats. To do so, it moves through the trees and simply reaches out and grabs the closest leaves!

The sloth slowly climbs down from its green paradise only once every week or so. On the ground, it moves at a speed of around 16 feet a minute. After descending a tree, it tidily relieves itself into a hole dug with its tail.

To escape danger, the sloth prefers to hide rather than run. A greenish algae grows on its fur—making for perfect camouflage in the jungle—and keeps the sloth from being spotted by predators during its long hours of sleep.

Central America

South America

Address: Central and South America

Size: From 19.5 to 23 inches long, plus a 3-inch-long tail

Weight: From 5 to 14 pounds

Favorite food: Leaves

The Cow

Lying in a pasture or on a bed of hay, the cow chews its cud 10 to 12 hours each day. Then it sleeps through the night!

During the summer, the cow spends nearly all its time chewing. First it pulls up clumps of grass by rolling them around its tongue. Then it swallows the clumps without chewing them. After swallowing a bellyful (sometimes as much as 100 pounds a day!), the cow lies down for a nap.

Inside the cow, the unchewed grass moves slowly through a series of four stomachs. Little by little, the grass softens up. Then the grass, or "cud," as it is now called, is regurgitated up from the stomach *back* into the cow's mouth! This time, the cow chews the cud before swallowing (and thoroughly digesting) it. A cow can chew its cud, or "ruminate," like this for 10 hours—without moving anything but its tail and ears to swat flies!

In the evening, after it has been milked, the cow is tired and says so by mooing. To rest up after its long day, it sleeps all night . . . and noisily expels gas! When it wakes, the cow's udder is full again and it needs to be milked. A single cow can produce between 6,000 and 8,000 quarts of milk a year—making this lazy herbivore *really* quite a productive one!

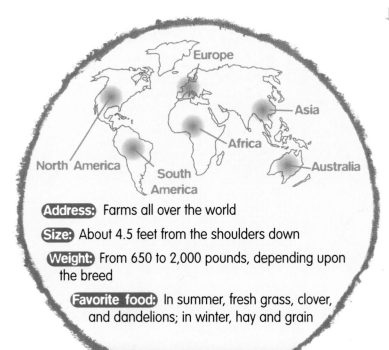

Europe
Asia
Africa
North America
South America
Australia

Address: Farms all over the world

Size: About 4.5 feet from the shoulders down

Weight: From 650 to 2,000 pounds, depending upon the breed

Favorite food: In summer, fresh grass, clover, and dandelions; in winter, hay and grain

Africa

Address: Rivers and lakes of Africa

Size: From 11 to 12 feet long

Weight: Male: About 3,500 to 7,000 pounds
Female: About 1,400 to 5,160 pounds

Favorite food: Herbs and other plants

The
Hippopotamus

As soon as the sun rises, the hippopotamus has to avoid the heat. Its hairless skin is very sensitive and needs to be covered for protection. Fortunately, the sweat from this massive creature acts like a sunscreen and protects it from burning. But even more protective—and fun—than sweating is bathing in muddy water! Mud sticks to the hippopotamus's skin and shields it from burning rays. It also helps to keep the horseflies and tsetse flies away.

A little friend comes in handy! One of the hippopotamus's best friends is the oxpecker. Perched on the hippo's back, the helpful bird pecks at the parasites on the hippo's skin.

While the sun beats down, the hippo—which is the heaviest land mammal after the elephant—spends its days soaking. It looks a bit like a submarine—only its ears, eyes, and nostrils are visible above the water. But the hippopotamus doesn't need a buoy to keep from sinking. It is wrapped in a 4-inch-thick layer of fat that keeps it afloat.

After a series of short naps on the water's surface, the lazy beast slides heavily into the swampy depths, where it can stay underwater for up to 5 minutes.

While in the water, the hippopotamus performs a very useful function. The excrement it releases into the water fertilizes the environment and helps microscopic plants and animals to grow. These microscopic organisms are the favorite food of young fish as well as other animals.

In the evening, when the sun goes down, swim time is over. Now the hippopotamus is hungry. In no hurry, it lumbers off to "mow" the savanna, eating up to 90 pounds of grass and other plants at every meal.

The hippopotamus rests all day submerged in the water . . . to keep from getting sunburned!

The cat

The domestic cat sleeps for 18 out of 24 hours and yawns at least 40 times a day!

Whatever the time of day or night, the cat loves to sleep. Whether in the sun or on its master's lap, the cat never misses an opportunity to take a catnap. It sleeps in two phases. First it sleeps deeply, almost without even moving its whiskers. This phase is called REM sleep. Then the cat begins to purr . . . and dream. It jerks its body and moves its paws. During this period, the cat's brain works as if it were awake.

Address: Everyplace inhabited by human beings

Size: Up to 3.5 feet long from the tip of the nose to the tip of the tail

Weight: From 4 to 16 pounds, depending upon the breed

Favorite food: Meat, fish, and poultry

To warm up its 600 muscles after each nap, the cat stretches its paws and raises its back until it forms a little bridge.

Then it's time to freshen up. The cat spends about 3 hours each day washing itself. It uses its front paws like a washcloth, covering them with saliva and rubbing them behind its head and ears. Because of its pivoting neck, the cat can lick its own back for a long time without losing its balance.

The cat uses its rough tongue to comb and clean its fur and remove loose hair. By licking itself, it absorbs bone-strengthening vitamin D from its fur. So the cat cleans itself and takes its vitamins at the same time. (How handy!)

Once it has finished napping and washing, the cat has only 3 short hours left to play!

The Garden Dormouse

Address: Europe, North Africa, and northwestern Russia

Size: From 3 to 7 inches long, plus a tail about 5 inches long

Weight: From 1.8 to almost 5 ounces

Favorite food: Snails, spiders, and fruit

This all-time sleep champion hibernates for up to 8 months a year.

This little rodent, which is identifiable by its mask of black fur around the eyes, thinks of nothing but sleep! Starting in September, the dormouse family climbs single file up tree trunks, ideally looking for an abandoned squirrel or bird's nest. They also climb mountain walls to hide among the rocks. Dormice are capable of living at altitudes of over 6,500 feet in the European Alps and the Pyrénées.

To prepare for their long sleep, dormice make cozy nests. On a mattress of grass, they make blankets from feathers and fur.

In groups of over 20 animals, the dormice will sleep curled into a ball throughout fall, winter, and half of spring, waking in May! Hungry little cannibals: the first dormouse to wake is so famished, it has been known to devour one of its sleeping friends—or relations!

Once its hibernation is over, the dormouse still spends its days sound asleep. At dusk, it wakes up, making squeaking noises that sound like birdcalls. Then it takes off to hunt spiders, baby birds, and snails. In the summertime, it is not unusual for dormice to invade people's pantries to gorge on nuts and fruit, then go to sleep amidst the canned goods, thinking it's fall while it's only mid-August!

In regions with cold winters, there are no mosquitoes or moths to eat from November to April. So, rather than starve, the lesser horseshoe bat saves its energy by sleeping all winter!

Nestled against its companions in a cave or other shelter, the bat hangs upside down by its claws and does not move a muscle. Its body can get so cold, drops of dew appear on its wings.

Come spring, hibernation ends and the bat goes back to work on the night shift. But the bat does not waste its time searching for insects. Instead, it finds them by making a sound that humans cannot hear, called ultrasound. This sound bounces off an insect and is echoed back to the bat. It does not even have to move its head to hear the sound because its ears can pivot by themselves!

Without moving a muscle, the bat can determine the precise distance between it and its prey. Once it has located its dinner, the bat unfolds its wings, swoops down, and makes its kill. After an exhausting night of eating insects, the bat will then sleep all day.

The Lesser Horseshoe Bat

When it hibernates, the bat is nearly frozen! Its body temperature—which is usually 102°F—can drop to 46°F!

Europe

Asia

North Africa

Persian Gulf

Address: Europe, North Africa, Asia, and the Persian Gulf region

Size: Wingspan from 7 to 10 inches long

Weight: From 4 to 10 grams

Favorite food: Flying insects

At top speed, this champion of slow motion moves at a rate of 30 feet an hour. The snail takes about 5 days to travel half a mile. . . .

The Edible Snail

Address: Europe

Size: From 2 to 4 inches long; shell from 2 to 3 inches long

Weight: About .8 ounce

Favorite food: Leaves, plant stems, and mushrooms

With just one foot, the edible snail—or escargot—is no marathon runner! To help it move a little faster, the snail produces a slime that helps it slide along more easily. This slime also helps protect the snail's foot from thorny plants and sharp objects in its path.

The snail doesn't need to move to drink. All it has to do is wait for rain. The snail then absorbs the water like a sponge. If a snail is exposed to the sun for too long, however, it can dry out and die of dehydration. To avoid this fate during the summer, the snail retracts into its shell and hangs out like that between rain showers.

When it eats, the snail takes several hours to swallow a piece of leaf. The snail cuts the leaf into little pieces using its tiny rough tongue, or "radula," which is covered with thousands of even tinier teeth!

In the fall, the edible snail disappears into the ground. It blocks the entrance to its shell by secreting saliva that is rich in lime and dries as hard as plaster. Nestled away like that, the snail will sleep for about 200 days—without eating or drinking—until spring.

With its head tucked into its pink feather pillow, the flamingo stands on one leg and sleeps without losing its balance!

The Flamingo

Address: The Caribbean, South America, southwestern Europe, Africa, and Asia

Size: From 4 to 5 feet high

Weight: From 4.5 to 7 pounds

Favorite food: Algae and crustaceans

When these elegant birds want to sleep, all they have to do is tuck their heads back over their shoulders and stand first on one leg, then on the other.

Eating isn't very difficult either. Thanks to their long, skinny legs, these flamingos can move through shallow ponds without getting their feathers wet. These stilt-like legs also help them to resist water currents without difficulty. They can remain motionless in the water for hours.

To fill up on their favorite foods, the hungry flamingos just have to poke their heads into the alkaline water. They let it flow into their beaks—which are equipped with thin blades that act like sieves—and filter algae and small crustaceans from the mud.

Flamingos swallow thousands of artemia, which are tiny shrimp. Natural pigments in these little shrimp help to deepen the pink of the flamingos' feathers!

Between April and early June is the breeding season. Flamingo parents incubate their egg with their legs folded over their mud nest. After 28 days, the baby flamingo hatches at last. Patiently, the father and mother beak-feed it with a pink porridge, or "milk," made of predigested stomach material. They also keep a careful eye out for predators such as seagulls, who would just love to dine on baby flamingos!

The Couch Potato Club

THE THREE-TOED
SLOTH

THE GARDEN
DORMOUSE

THE HIPPOPOTAMUS

THE ORANGUTAN

THE ALPINE
MARMOT

THE BROWN BEAR

THE COW

THE LESSER
HORSESHOE BAT

THE CAT

THE GRASS SNAKE

THE EDIBLE SNAIL

THE FLAMINGO

Know someone
who should
join this club?
Paste his or her
picture here!

Know someone
who should
join this club?
Paste his or her
picture here!

Photographs:
Brown bear: Y. Noto Campanella/BIOS.
Orangutan: left, C. Ruoso/BIOS; cover and interior right, Seitre/BIOS.
Grass snake: K. H. Jacobi/OKAPIA/BIOS.
Alpine marmot: left, C. Ruoso/BIOS; right, T. Roig/BIOS.
Three-toed sloth: M. Fogden/O.S.F./BIOS.
Cow: D. Halleux/BIOS.
Hippopotamus: R. de la Harpe/BIOS.
Cat: J. J. Alcalay/BIOS.
Garden dormouse: D. Heuclin/BIOS.
Lesser horseshoe bat: J. Robert/JACANA.
Edible snail: top left, N. Petit/BIOS; bottom, B. Renevey/BIOS.
Flamingo: F. Marquez/BIOS.

First American edition, 2002

Library of Congress Cataloging-in-Publication Data
Doinet, Mymi. The laziest / [Mymi Doinet].
  p. cm. — (Faces of nature)
ISBN 0-375-81408-6
1. Sleep behavior in animals—Juvenile literature. [1. Animals—Sleep behavior.
2. Animals—Habits and behavior.]
I. Title. QL755.3 .D65 2002 591.5'19—dc21 2001019275

www.randomhouse.com/kids

Printed in Malaysia February 2002 10 9 8 7 6 5 4 3 2 1
RANDOM HOUSE and colophon are registered trademarks of Random House, Inc.